LET'S PLAY! LITTLE CHAMPS

FLAG FOOTBALL

RYAN JAMES

NorwoodHouse Press

Library of Congress Cataloging-in-Publication Data

Names: James, Ryan.
Title: Flag football / Ryan James.
Description: Buffalo, NY : Norwood House Press, 2025. | Series: Let's play! little champs | Includes glossary and index.
Identifiers: ISBN 9781684502264 (pbk.) | ISBN 9781684502271 (library bound) | ISBN 9781684502288 (ebook)
Subjects: LCSH: Flag football--Juvenile literature.
Classification: LCC GV952.2 J359 2025 | DDC 796.332'8--dc23

Published in 2025 by
Norwood House Press
2544 Clinton Street
Buffalo, NY 14224

Designer: Ocean Books
Editor: Kim Thompson

Photo credits: Cover, pp. 1, 5, 7, 11, 12, 15, 16, 19 JoeSAPhotos/Shutterstock.com; p. 6 Reel creative/Shutterstock.com; p. 8 sportoakimirka/Shutterstock.com; p. 17 Stuart Monk/Shutterstock.com; p. 21 Rawpixel.com/Shutterstock.com

Printed in the United States of America

TABLE OF CONTENTS

What Is Flag Football?

Flag football is a fun and safe game. In regular football, you stop the person who is carrying the football by **tackling** them. In flag football, you stop them by pulling a **flag** off their belt.

The Uniform

Players wear a belt that has flags attached by Velcro. The flags hang down, so they are easy to grab.

Players also wear **lightweight** jerseys and shorts. They wear cleats on their feet to help them run on the grass.

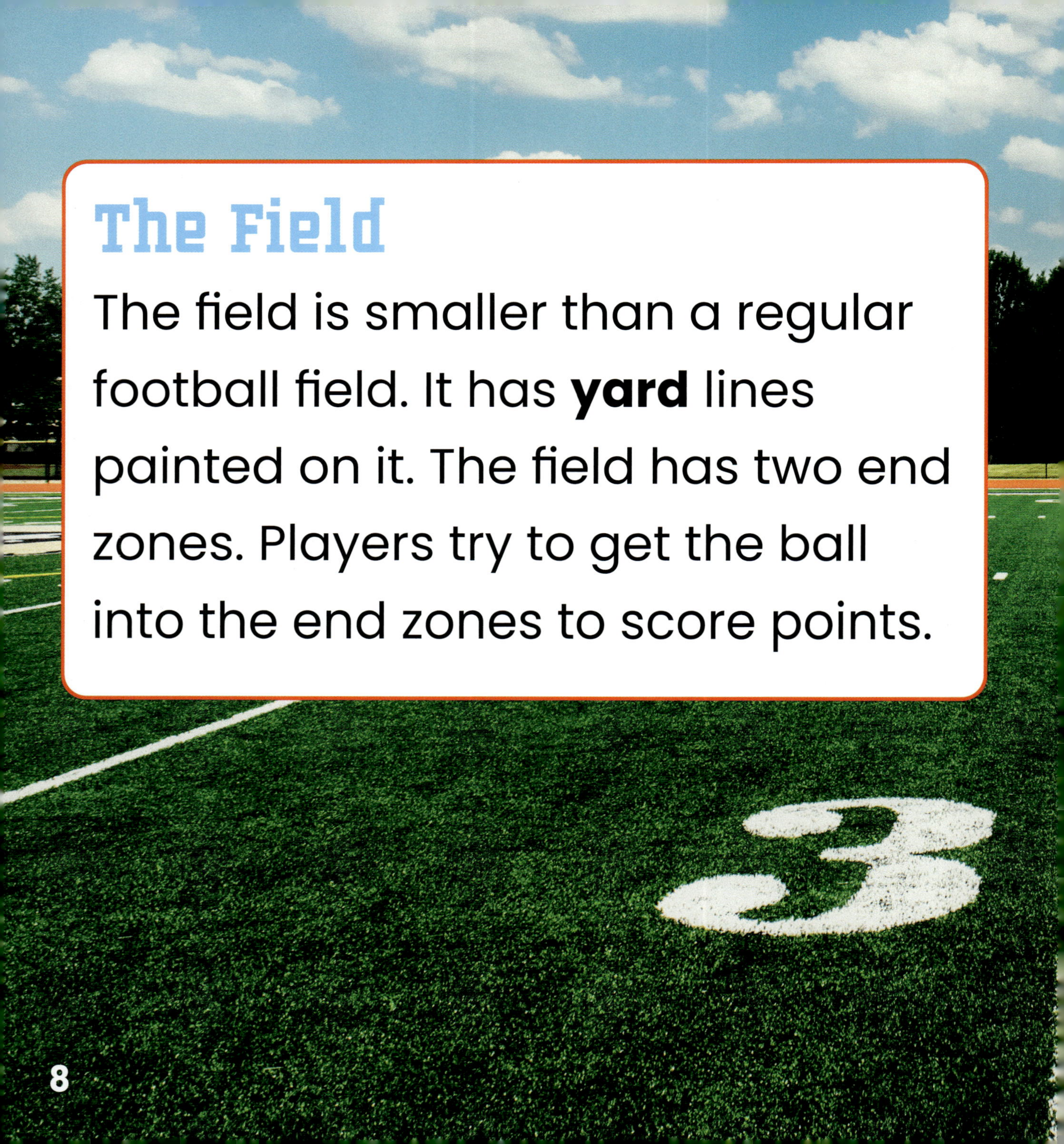

The Field

The field is smaller than a regular football field. It has **yard** lines painted on it. The field has two end zones. Players try to get the ball into the end zones to score points.

Rules of the Game

The game starts with a **kickoff**. One team kicks the football to the other team. The receiving team tries to move the ball forward by running with it or passing it.

The **opposing** team tries to stop the players who have the ball. When a player's flag is pulled from their belt, they must stop.

Each team tries to score by moving the ball all the way forward into the other team’s end zone. This is called a touchdown, and it is worth six points.

Positions on the Team

There are many positions on a team. Players on offense try to score. The quarterback throws the football to other players and sometimes runs with it.

The center **snaps** the football to the quarterback at the start of each play.

The wide receiver catches passes from the quarterback.

The running back takes handoffs from the quarterback and runs forward with the ball.

Players on defense try to block the other team from scoring. The safety tries to pull the flag of the player who is carrying the ball.

The linebacker tries to make the ball carrier run out of bounds.

How to Be Game-Ready

Players should eat healthy foods like fruits, vegetables, and lean meats. They should drink plenty of water. Getting enough sleep gives them **energy** to run and play.

GLOSSARY

energy (EN-ur-jee): the ability to do work

flag (flag): the material that hangs down from a flag football player's belt and that is pulled off to stop the ball carrier

kickoff (KIK-awf): a kick of the ball that starts the action in a flag football game

lightweight (LITE-wayt): not weighing very much; easy to move

opposing (uh-POH-zing): opposite; playing for the team you are trying to beat

snaps (snaps): passes the football backward to the quarterback to start a play

tackling (TAK-ling): forcing a player to fall to the ground

yard (yahrd): a distance equal to three feet or 36 inches (91 centimeters)

THINKING QUESTIONS

1. What are the parts of a flag football player's uniform?

2. Why is the safety an important player on a flag football team?

3. How is flag football different from regular football?

4. Why do flag football players need to eat healthy foods?

5. What qualities do you think a good flag football player has?

INDEX

ABOUT THE AUTHOR

Ryan James lives in the western part of North Carolina with his rescue dog Bailey. As a child, he would search for creepy crawlies as he hiked through the forest near his house. When he's not on the hiking or biking trail, he is cheering on his favorite baseball and football teams.